LIVING IN
THE FOREST

LIVING IN THE FOREST

CONTEMPORARY HOUSES IN THE WOODS

[1] BUILT TO FRAME THE FOREST

THE FOREST 7
[2] BUILT IN HARMONY WITH THE FOREST 91
[3] BUILT TO BECOME THE FOREST

Given the many scientific studies that point to the healing properties of trees, it's no wonder so many people dream of finding a little corner of woodland to call home. Forests are the ultimate antidote to the ever-quickening pace of daily life, as well as the rapid urbanization of our environments: they can clean our air, soothe our minds, and even boost our immune systems. So keenly felt are the benefits of spending time among the trees that, in the 1980s, a practice emerged in Japan called *shinrin-yoku*, or forest bathing. Underpinned by government research, *shinrin-yoku* became a recognized form of ecotherapy, providing relief from stress and reminding people of the importance of protecting the country's forests.

As forward-thinking as it might have sounded at the time, the concept of forest bathing merely formalized something that human beings have understood for centuries: nature is a tonic. Take nineteenth-century American naturalist Henry David Thoreau—who went to live at Walden Pond in Massachusetts to pursue a simpler existence—and the people of Plum Village Buddhist monastery, an internationally renowned center for mindfulness that's nestled in French woodland, as two examples. But, as built environments steadily encroach on natural ones, it's clear that not everyone strives to live in such harmony with the land—and one can't help but wonder at the cost.

Fortunately, as this book outlines, many of those who seek the solace of a forest sanctuary go to great lengths to preserve their surroundings. They track down like-minded architects, who in turn look for ever-more-inventive ways of building conscientiously and sustainably. From tiny off-grid tree houses to experimental passive architecture, the designs that follow proffer a myriad of ways to respect and reconnect with nature—whether built within a biosphere reserve or, more surprisingly, in the middle of a city.

Divided into three chapters, the fifty projects contained in this book are shining examples of biophilic architecture. The first group of houses emphasizes the majestic beauty of the wooded landscape, using carefully framed views and considered layouts to showcase the best of the scenery. In the second chapter, you'll discover a collection of homes that integrate seamlessly into the forest. They harness natural materials and take all manner of different forms to exist harmoniously within their habitats. The third section showcases projects that test the limits of building in the wilderness. The architects of these residences have tackled isolated locations and challenging sites to design spaces that offer an immersive experience of forest living.

Whether flanked by towering pines, enveloped by the jungle, built into a shoreline, or perched on a mountainside, these dwellings offer a multitude of different takes on the archetypal forest refuge. Inspired by folklore, indigenous culture, vernacular architecture, or the land itself, many of their designers have drawn from the past to create homes for the future. In doing so, these architects have melded tradition with innovation to break new ground in sustainable construction, reframing the way we live in nature.

[1] BUILT TO FRAME THE FOREST

An increasing amount of research points to the physical and mental benefits offered by viewing green spaces large and small, from improving air quality to providing relief for harried and overstimulated minds. It's even thought that just a few minutes spent casting your eyes over pictures of trees can help to counteract the effects of chronic stress. Imagine, then, the restorative potential of actually living in a home with wraparound forest views or uninterrupted sight lines across verdant treetops.

When designing a home in a wooded location, one of the most pivotal decisions for architects is how best to capitalize on the spectacular natural backdrop. Positioning and layout are key, as illustrated by the houses in this chapter, many of which feature abstract forms and unconventional floor plans that respond to the challenging topography of their sites. Staggered planes and fragmented volumes allow surrounding vegetation to go untouched, creating leafy screens that remain visible throughout interior spaces. Stilted foundations elevate buildings to improve their vantage points and to reduce the impact of construction on the land.

Some of the houses in the following pages were revised multiple times in order to navigate—and protect—the densely forested plots on which they sit. In other cases, environmental constraints became a creative springboard for experimental contemporary designs. A common thread that connects them all is an architect's expert eye for framing. These structures share elements such as expansive apertures, walls of floor-to-ceiling windows, and retractable doors that peel spaces open to emphasize their outlook. Some clever touches include strips of glass in floors that showcase foliage beneath, and skylights that extend from ceilings to walls to outline views of trees and sky.

Serene interiors flow out onto generous decks and terraces that extend to meet the views. Many of the dwellings possess a pavilion-like quality, with enclosed spaces positioned in the center or to the rear, enabling living areas to remain open to the elements and to offer panoramic scenery. Inside these tranquil forest retreats, minimalist design abounds, deliberately encouraging the eye to be drawn outward to the impressive landscapes.

TOFINO BEACH HOUSE

2021 | Vancouver Island, BC, Canada

Encased in glass and surrounded by greenery, this secluded Canadian home is located in Tofino's coastal forest, part of Vancouver Island's Pacific Rim National Park Reserve. A wall of floor-to-ceiling windows in the main living space frames dramatic views of the ocean, which is just a stone's throw from the house, while slatted timber cladding to the rear creates a feeling of sanctuary. The tall trees, visible on all sides, contribute to this comforting effect.

The 2,500-square-foot (232-square-meter) single-story dwelling is the work of Seattle-based practice Olson Kundig, which is renowned for clean-lined, considered architecture that sits in harmony with the natural landscape. Here, the firm opted for a cantilevered construction to provide an area for ferns and coastal shrubs to grow beneath the house. The foliage is visible through glass flooring that runs around the perimeter of the open-plan kitchen, dining, and living area, creating the illusion of floating above the forest floor.

Inside, a material palette of wood and concrete strengthens the home's connection to its rugged surroundings; two fireplaces, one at either end of the main space, emphasize a sense of refuge. The warm and textural interior features bespoke furniture, including sleek walnut seating built into one of the hearths, by principal architect and founding partner Jim Olson. Pieces from the owner's collection of contemporary art provide pops of color that punctuate the pared-back interior design scheme, but the real spectacle is the sight of waves and wild beaches beyond the trees.

Hidden away in the remote Primavera Forest, just outside the city of Guadalajara in Mexico, this concrete house is so well camouflaged within the craggy, wooded landscape that it is barely visible between the trees. The two-level structure is built into the hillside. Its abstract form is a response to the challenging topography of the site, as well as a strategy to preserve as much of the surrounding vegetation as possible.

Architect René Pérez Gómez of an eponymous local studio wanted the building to seem as if it were emerging from the earth, so he designed the house to look like an extension of the ground beneath it. The lower level of the home contains the living spaces, with a separate wing for the kitchen, dining area, and main bedroom; the upper level comprises expansive roof terraces and a small garden.

The concrete exterior is deliberately stripped back, in order to blur the boundary between where the house ends and the forest begins. Open stairs connect the levels, and the architecture's striking outline has a Brutalist quality. In keeping with the home's no-frills form, the interior is equally pared back: the usual accoutrements of day-to-day living are distilled to the barest essentials. For the architect, this was a deliberate strategy to simplify the life of the home's inhabitants and encourage reflection and connection with each other and with the forest.

Positioned on a 2 acre (1 hectare) plot that's hidden away in the Sierra Nevada, this California home is a low-lying two-story structure built from wood, concrete, steel, and glass. Surrounded by a forest of lofty pine and fir trees, the house is situated in Martis Valley on the outskirts of Truckee, a small town close to the north shore of Lake Tahoe.

For the exterior of the building, local firm Faulkner Architects drew inspiration from traditional timber construction techniques but used fire-resistant materials: board-formed concrete and slatted screens made from ebony-colored steel. This contemporary take on vernacular mountain architecture protects the wood-framed elements of the house from the threat of wildfires.

With its south-facing aspect, the 4,500-square-foot (418-square-meter) home is perfectly positioned to collect solar energy throughout the year. A radiant heating system and enhanced glazing add to its energy efficiency. Inside, a cohesive material palette—reclaimed teak ceilings and floors, white gypsum, and more board-formed concrete—creates a warm, harmonious ambience.

Green-glass screens mark the entrance to the house, providing a pop of verdant color that nods to the evergreen forest outside. Beyond these, an open-plan living, dining, and kitchen area unfolds, where a wall of sliding doors connects the space to a generous sheltered terrace outside. Huge skylights extend from the roof down to the walls, allowing light to flood in during the day and providing views of the stars at night.

When San José, Costa Rica–based practice Studio Saxe embarked on this project in Santa Teresa—a small beach town on Costa Rica's Nicoya Peninsula—the architects' first task was to decide how best to integrate the house into the lush jungle on the waterfront plot. The studio's solution was to design the home as a series of pavilions, with extended, overlapping roofs that soften the exterior lines of the architecture and help it blend in with the surroundings.

Expanses of glass give this sprawling 10,764-square-foot (1,000-square-meter) residence an air of lightness, which is enhanced by a series of thin steel columns that support the slender roof planes. Beneath these, serene interior spaces flow out onto the pool deck and surrounding terraces, blurring the boundaries between inside and out. Jungle foliage springs up amid the structures, peeking out between rooms and enveloping the building in greenery.

Glazed corridors link the pavilions—which are divided into bedrooms, living spaces, and service areas—ensuring that the jungle remains visible at all times. In addition, every room features glass doors on two or three sides that connect to the outdoors, enabling the cooling ocean breeze to circulate throughout the house.

Underpinned by passive architectural principles, the house was informed by a bioclimatic design process that analyzes weather patterns to minimize energy usage. The overhanging roofs cleverly protect the house from the sun and the rain, while a thoughtful combination of eco-friendly systems, such as rainwater catchment and energy generation, make this project a pioneer in sustainable tropical architecture.

This Canadian home's narrow plot prompted a clever design solution from Montreal-based firm Natalie Dionne Architecture. Elevated on stilts, the house straddles two rocky outcrops. It is located in Quebec's Eastern Townships region, a popular vacation destination for Montrealers. The owners of the home had long wished to live in a woodland retreat, so they purchased some land in the area on which to build.

For the architects, finding the right spot within the rugged 3 acre (1 hectare) site wasn't easy. Unafraid of a challenge, they opted for a shallow ravine, which is surrounded by trees and bathed in natural light. In response to the topography, the studio came up with a bridge-like design that raised the house 10 feet (3 meters) above the ground and stretched it between the two rocky embankments.

The striking, slender abode has a pleasing geometric feel. The staggered exterior is softened with the use of graying white cedar, which the architects had treated with an ageing accelerator to speed up the natural weathering process. The interiors combine blond, bleached, and grizzled wood, with solid maple kitchen counters and built-in furniture made from Russian plywood. Light pours in from all sides, causing the forest outside to cast dappled shadows across the polished concrete floors. Huge picture windows frame the treetops in the valley below, while a covered terrace stretches out toward the tree line.

In a tree-lined clearing on the Danish island of Fyn, this house was built for a young family after a fire destroyed their previous residence. Villa Korup's unusual three-winged formation was designed by Danish-German firm Jan Henrik Jansen Arkitekter, in collaboration with Australian architect Marshall Blecher. The home is made of cross-laminated timber clad in raw weathering steel. The sustainable, FSC-certified Baltic fir panels used in the construction were robotically manufactured off site. This meant that, amazingly, the house took just three days to erect.

The unique shape of the design creates three separate zones within the leafy plot: a sunny sloped area to the south, a sheltered kitchen garden to the east, and an orchard playground for the children to the west. Inside, the arrangement provides convivial communal spaces for the family to gather, as well as more secluded areas for privacy and contemplation at the tips of the building's wings, which stretch out to meet the trees that encircle the plot.

The exterior of the house was designed to evolve over time, allowing it to blend into the woodland around it. The custom-designed steel cladding system reacts to the weather, turning from an oily metallic gray to a deep, earthy umber. The timber interior was treated with soap and lye, in the traditional Danish manner, which protects the wood and gives it a soft yet resilient finish. The result is an experimental island home that is a sleek, geometric addition to the forest landscape.

This hillside home makes creative use of its tricky sloping site in a densely forested plot in southwest Iceland's Thingvellir National Park. KRADS, a studio based in Denmark and Iceland, conceived the house's black timber design. Led by cofounders Kristján Eggertsson and Kristján Örn Kjartansson, the practice reimagines Nordic architecture and design.

The architects carefully considered the choice of the house's site. The location they selected allows the house to assimilate into the surrounding landscape and to frame breathtaking views of the vast lake to the north and mountains to the south. In order to negotiate the rugged volcanic terrain, the building's concrete foundation is made up of three staggered planes that follow the formation of the hillside. Preserving the natural landscape was the main goal in both the design and construction process. As such, the land surrounding the house is so thick with trees that it is practically impenetrable, and the sloping green roof echoes the outline of the hillside.

Overgrown with grass and moss, the roof forms a perfect viewing platform that's accessible from the home's upper level or from the base of the slope outside. The building's highest point is the perfect place to take in the landscape's ever-changing panorama. Inside, spaces are imbued with Scandinavian simplicity; a tranquil white-and-wood scheme encourages the eye to focus outward toward water, trees, and sky.

Featuring a laid-back interior with expansive openings that connect the home to the outdoors on all sides, this Mexican home is the ultimate beach retreat. Situated close to the ocean in Tulum, on the Yucatán Peninsula, Casa Areca's architecture and landscaping are by nearby design office CO-LAB. The architects positioned the home strategically within its narrow plot, in order to maintain the natural screen of areca palms and other tropical plants that offer shade as well as privacy for the house and its tranquil pool area.

Upstairs, four en-suite bedrooms benefit from large windows that allow the coastal breeze to flow throughout. Below, an airy open-plan living area features pivoting and retractable glazed doors that can open up the space on two sides, fusing the ground floor with a sizable deck outside. The home's careful placement preserves the trees that cover the plot, creating a luxuriant garden. Stone that was salvaged during the pool construction has been used to build the wall surrounding the property, providing a rugged backdrop to the pool and densely planted outdoor space.

The house itself is constructed from concrete blocks and reinforced concrete, with walls and floors finished in polished cement. A solar panel system has been put in place and much of the furniture was designed by CO-LAB and built by Yucatán artisans from locally harvested wood. The architects chose to treat the timber so that it tones beautifully with the pure and natural interior palette, which helps to anchor the home in its beachside location.

YOO FOREST HOUSE

2021 | Cotswolds, England, UK

A minimalist dwelling inspired by the pioneering designs of German architect Ludwig Mies van der Rohe and his contemporaries, this English woodland escape is part of the Lakes by Yoo, a 650 acre (263 hectare) development of contemporary country homes in the Cotswolds. The Gloucestershire house was designed by British design firm Broadway Malyan, who were commissioned to build a single-story residence with a Modernist aesthetic on the rural site.

Unlike the lakeside houses in the development, Yoo Forest House is on a grassy plot completely enclosed by trees. The pavilion-like home has glass walls on three sides. The rectilinear structure is an arresting sight within the leafy setting, its strong horizontal planes contrasting with the vertical lines of the tall, slim trunks of the adjacent birch trees. The surrounding woodland forms a natural barrier around the house, ensuring privacy for its guests and allowing the architects to imbue the building with its characteristic transparency and less-is-more aesthetic.

The interior is designed to flow out effortlessly into the verdant garden. The facade facing the lawn is made up of a number of glass doors that connect the interior to an elevated exterior platform, which appears to float just above the ground. Below this, a narrow stream cascades gently down a series of steps, adding the sound of trickling water to the calming rustle of the wind in the trees. The architects used slatted timber around the doors, beneath the roof overhang, and to the rear of the sleek home, in keeping with the sylvan location.

Alexander Gorlin Architects
STERLING FOREST HOUSE
2021 | Hudson Valley, NY, USA

In this project, the clients asked Alexander Gorlin Architects to create a bold and contemporary residence in New York's Hudson Valley, in a village famed for its historic nineteenth-century architecture. In addition, the house needed to offer privacy for its owners and cause minimal disturbance to the wooded surroundings. To fulfill all those objectives, the New York practice chose locally quarried stone for the structure's boxy exterior and built the house into a rocky shelf on the hillside plot.

Restricting the building's environmental impact became integral to the design process. A large proportion of the site was left untouched, allowing the wildness of the landscape to remain front and center. The architects adjusted both the house's location and layout several times to reduce the number of trees that needed to be removed from the plot. Adding a green roof offset any vegetation lost during construction.

The L-shaped building is centered around an internal rock garden, and an exterior of pink and gray granite ensures that the house is an unobtrusive addition to the hillside. To maximize time spent in the fresh air, a cantilevered glass canopy juts out from the roof, providing shelter for the outdoor areas during inclement weather. The kitchen, dining area, and living spaces all flow out onto an elevated deck, beneath which are peaceful private terraces that lead off each of the bedrooms and look out to the trees.

Surrounded by thick jungle, this pair of Costa Rican houses is walking distance from the Pacific Ocean. Local architecture firm Studio Saxe designed the side-by-side homes to look like a series of modules, with portions of the buildings left completely open, thus blending the tropical rainforest into their design. Flat, pavilion-like roofs with deep overhangs connect spaces and shelter the outdoor areas from sun and rain.

The buildings' exteriors feature decorative wooden screens that partially enclose some spaces. The smaller of the two beach homes is set across one story but shares the same architectural language as the bigger house, which has two floors, a double-height living area, and overreaching rooflines. The houses' communal zones are structurally supported by black-painted steel frames that have a lightweight appearance, keep the spaces open to the elements, and contrast with the backdrop of greenery. More private areas, such as the bedrooms and bathrooms, are tucked away inside solid concrete volumes.

Cross ventilation, as well as the abundance of natural light that permeates the buildings, keeps energy usage to a minimum. All hot water is generated by each home's solar panels, and the vast flat roofs collect the water to irrigate the gardens. Reforested teak was used for both the roofs and the screens, which allow ocean breezes to flow through the houses and cast dappled shadows on the glossy polished concrete floors. For the interiors, Studio Saxe enlisted interior designer Cristina de Freitas, who created a fresh and simple scheme that feels in keeping with the tropical setting.

When the owners of this second home decided they wanted to spend more time in their peaceful forest retreat, they turned to RAMA Estudio to expand and renovate the space. To achieve this, the Quito, Ecuador–based practice designed a metal-frame extension that hovers over the hillside, adding a further 1,292-square-feet (120-square-meters) to the 700-square-foot (65-square-meter) residence, which is in Ecuador's northern Sierra region. Designed with a minimum foundation to avoid impact on the land beneath, the prefabricated structure was manufactured and assembled in less than three months, and it is topped with a green roof for thermal insulation.

Encased in tempered glass, the extension is enveloped by views of a lush valley where a screen of trees creates a secluded sanctuary. At its center is a double-sided storage unit that partitions the space, serving the kitchen on one side and the living area on the other. Another wall of storage marks the boundary between the extension and the original house, which now benefits from a reconfigured floor plan, multifunctional furniture, and larger windows that make more of the home's forest location.

A restrained interior palette of plywood and metal allows the trees outside to take center stage, while thoughtful additions, such as a desk mounted onto one of the floor-to-ceiling windows, capitalize on the verdant views. Underfloor heating and an open fire keep the home warm in winter, despite the expanses of glass, so the family can enjoy an escape to the woods at any time of year.

From afar, this concrete structure on Mexico's Yucatán Peninsula could almost be mistaken for a disused industrial building, where nature has been slowly and steadily working to reclaim the plot. In fact, it's a contemporary home designed by Mexico City architecture firm Productora, which was tasked with designing a beach house on a narrow strip of land in Quintana Roo on the Riviera Maya. Partially hidden within the jungle of the protecting buffer zone surrounding Sian Ka'an Biosphere Reserve in Tulum, the residence nestles its L-shaped plan closely around the trees that cover this section of coast.

Powered entirely by wind and solar energy, the building is cast in a pigmented concrete that reacts to the sun over time, taking on shades ranging from blue to pink. Its foundation is raised up on cross-shaped columns, reducing damage to the landscape and creating views over a broad dune that separates the house from the shoreline. Despite its elevated design, the structure is largely concealed by jungle vegetation, with trailing plants tracing the line of the rooftop pool terrace. From here, a sweeping spiral staircase descends through the core of the building, connecting its three levels.

The main living quarters are located on the middle floor, where folding louvred doors connect the interior with wooden decking on both sides. These terraces are shaded by awnings, made of local wood, that can be lowered to offer robust protection in the event of hurricanes and tropical storms. At the far end of the L-shaped plan, a distinctive turret-like structure is situated close to the main bedroom, providing a flexible space for work or meditation overlooking the jungle canopy and the Caribbean Sea.

PUNTA CHILEN

2021 | Chiloé, Chile

A bold red building that mimics a tree house with its raised design, this timber extension was created to develop an existing home on the Chilean island of Chiloé by Santiago-based studio Guillermo Acuña Arquitectos Asociados. The extension is positioned at the mouth of the Chacao Channel, across the water from mainland Chile, and it rests on tall pine stilts that bring it level with the canopy of the adjacent forest. The vertical stilts echo the lines of the tree trunks, while the slanted posts provide additional support for the extension, which occupies an exposed spot on the small peninsula of Punta Chilen.

The traditional fishermen's houses of Castro informed the extension's elevated design, which keeps the building above water level, even at high tide. Helping to embed the building into the forest, red-painted outdoor decks and walkways extend out into the wooded shoreline and around a solitary tree. Inspired by the red shade used to paint lighthouses, Guillermo Acuña and his team chose the bright color to make the home stand out from the landscape.

Inside, a huge U-shaped banquette defines a living and dining space that's bounded by glass on three sides, framing ocean views. At its center are three indoor grills with funnel-shaped chimneys that extend up through the roof, and a generous dining table. In the slatted pine kitchen, open shelving lines the windows in place of concealed storage, allowing the landscape to remain ever present, with the beach and trees visible between the shelves.

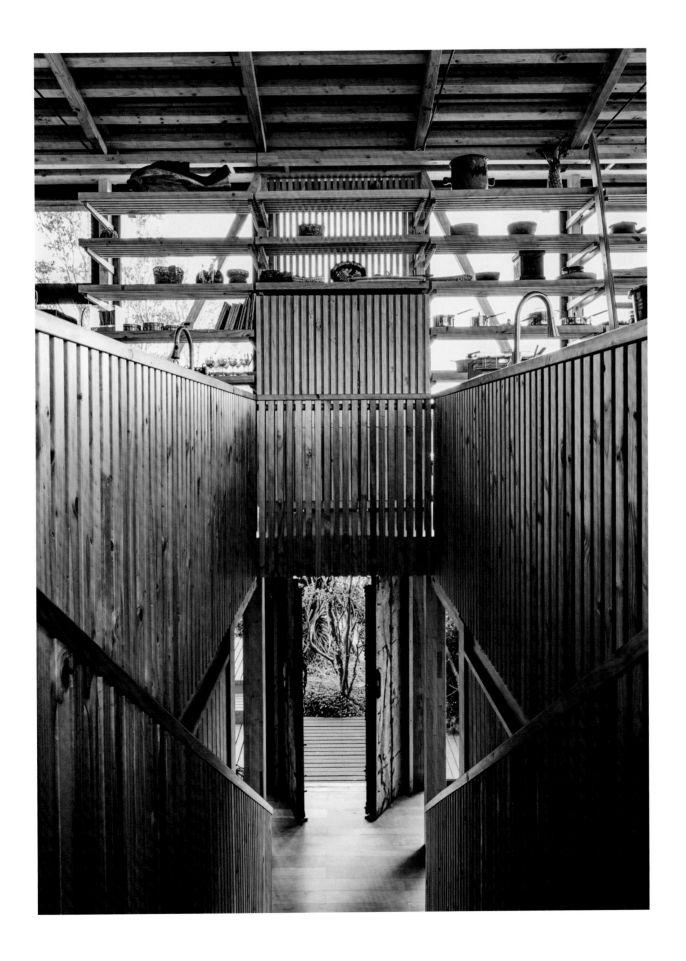

This gleaming white Bangkok residence is home to not only a family of seven, but also a forest of more than 120 trees. Local landscape architecture firm Shma, which specializes in green infrastructure, designed the striking structure. It conceived the experimental concept as a way to combat climate change, improve air quality, and counteract rapid urbanization in the densely populated city.

Aptly named Forest House, the project responds to a trend of replacing smaller homes with buildings of increasing size, thus sacrificing much-needed green space on their plots. As a result, neighborhoods are becoming more urban and less healthy, deprived of clean air as well as nature. Designed as a series of adjacent segments, every roof surface of this house has been used for planting vegetation, with trees growing up between the three volumes. Giant planters have also been integrated into the home's upper levels, with greenery providing a natural screen for the street-facing bedrooms. Despite the amount of foliage surrounding the house, the interior is filled with light, due to two internal courtyards that separate the blocks.

More than twenty indigenous species of trees can be found on and around the building. The mix includes evergreen and flowering trees, creating a biodiverse environment for insects and other wildlife all year round. Shma chose the species for their minimal water requirements and their shapes, so the firm could accommodate as much vegetation as possible on the site. A fruit and vegetable garden thrives on the sun-drenched roof, providing food security for the family, while the dense foliage helps boost oxygen levels for the surrounding area.

Peeping out from the trees on a rocky shoreline in the San Juan Islands, this coastal retreat is so discreet, boaters could sail right by without noticing it. Located on Orcas Island in northern Washington, the house was conceived by Seattle studio Heliotrope Architects, whose aim was to create a design that blended in with the wooded coastline and minimized exposure to the weather.

To this end, the one-level house is sited in a dip between the rocks and clad in timber shingles that have been treated to match the gray tones of the craggy landscape and the bark of adjacent fir trees. Walls of wooden shutters can be drawn along the perimeters of the house to protect each glass facade from the area's harsh winter storms. In good weather, these shutters can be pulled back, connecting the central living area to the sea on one side and the forest on the other.

Because the site is within the protected San Juan Islands National Monument, the architects had to avoid damaging both the shoreline and the marine environment. In order to minimize its impact on the delicate ecosystem, the house was topped with a garden roof that replaced the land that was lost during construction. The design involved native wood, such as Douglas fir and western red cedar; Heliotrope's architects recruited local craftspeople to assist with the construction. The result is a beautifully made, sympathetically designed home in tune to the unique conditions of the shoreline forest.

This Tennessee home is situated in the foothills of the French Broad River Basin, with views through the forest to the Great Smoky Mountains. Designed by Sanders Pace Architecture, a practice based in nearby Knoxville, the house is comprised of three separate pavilions connected by a metal roof that zigzags across the structures. The home's unconventional formation twists to follow the ridge on which it sits, making use of a clearing in a grove of native hardwoods.

One of the pavilions houses an open-plan kitchen, dining area, and living room, another contains two bedrooms, and the remaining volume serves as a garage. Between them, sheltered by the thin plane of the roof, are voids that serve as porch areas offering distinct views of both the forest and the mountains. Cementitious fiberboard panels cover much of the exterior, which is painted in shades of burnt orange and russet; the colors were inspired by the autumnal tones that surrounded the architects on their first visit to the site.

Full-height windows are set at intervals along the side of the building, strategically positioned to provide different outlooks to the forest and to moderate the natural light that beams into the interior. Stained cypress wood breaks up the bold swathes of orange paneling in the facade, providing an all-season link to the surrounding trees. Behind the bright facade is a simple, neutral scheme that's refined and honest. White walls and whitewashed oak floors contribute to the airiness of the spaces, while the many windows inject color from the woodland foliage outside.

[2]   BUILT IN HARMONY WITH THE FOREST

Twentieth-century German architect Ludwig Mies van der Rohe, whose influential designs were integral to the evolution of Modernist architecture, once remarked, "Nature, too, shall live its own life. We must beware not to disrupt it with the color of our houses and interior fittings. Yet we should attempt to bring nature, houses, and human beings together into a higher unity." The homes that follow embody this sentiment entirely, drawing on techniques old and new to help them assimilate harmoniously into their surroundings.

Whether sitting lightly on the land, embedded into the landscape, or suspended high up in the trees, the foundations of these buildings often form the starting point for their overall design. Some of the structures, such as one prefabricated home on a rented plot in a Dutch forest, are designed to leave no trace at all once dismantled. Others, like the Norwegian tree house that's fastened to a living tree trunk, barely impact the environment at all.

The houses in this chapter take on all manner of forms to integrate seamlessly into their sylvan habitats. Low-slung, linear abodes crouch unassumingly beneath leafy canopies, spear-shaped structures extend upward and outward to meet the trees, angular plans trace the contours of hillside clearings, and sculptural dwellings weave themselves around ancient trunks. A select palette of timber, stone, and clay roots these homes to the land and allows the buildings to blend in with their surroundings. Locally sourced materials, such as native hardwoods, play a vital part in much of these houses' construction.

Garden roofs and cascades of greenery offer additional camouflage, offsetting building footprints with expansive planted surfaces. Additional methods used to soften edges and boundaries include thatched canopies, slatted sunshades, and louvred screens, which draw from a mix of traditional and progressive building techniques. Inside, the focus remains outdoors, with swaths of glass or open-sided volumes helping each project to stay connected to the landscape. Restrained interiors harness nature's timeless appeal and foster a close relationship with the forest.

Composed of five freestanding volumes spread out beneath a rustic slatted pergola, designed by Marcio Kogan's studio, this house occupies a verdant and sandy plot overlooking the Atlantic Ocean in Brazil's northeast region. Kogan's practice, Studio MK27, experimented with dissolving conventional architectural boundaries in the project, which plays with light and shadow and weaves tropical trees into the fabric of its design.

A spacious, raised outdoor deck links the kitchen, dining room, living space, and bedrooms, all of which are contained within the separate structures, with a wall of greenery visible in between. According to the architects, the deck acts as the home's "connective tissue," taking the place of internal corridors and walkways. This ensures that inhabitants spend as much time outside as possible, taking in the surrounding nature and the sound of the ocean.

The eucalyptus pergola that covers the entire deck is supported by a series of laminated wooden frames. To soften the line between architecture and nature, the architects designed both the deck and pergola around the mature forest that covers this beachside lot in Trancoso, Bahia. This created openings for sunlight to pour into across the various outdoor spaces, while tree branches provide additional shade overhead.

An inviting swimming pool acts as a bridge between the house and the beach, mimicking a natural body of water with its organic, palm-fringed form. Its curved design is also one of many Modernist references that can be seen outside and in, such as the home's low-lying, linear facade and its considered selection of midcentury furniture, lighting, and art.

This compact A-frame chalet occupies a prime location on a tree-covered mountainside in Donovaly, a popular ski resort in Slovakia's Low Tatras National Park. Y100 ateliér, an architecture studio based in nearby Banská Bystrica, recently renovated and remodeled the glass-fronted structure, which dates back to the 1970s.

The studio's brief was to make the 570-square-foot (53-square-meter) chalet more livable for its owners. The architects updated the floor plan while ensuring the remodeled interior made the most of the unspoiled forest views. Their first task was to remove a first-floor bedroom, in order to create a double-height living-dining space that benefits from the floor-to-ceiling triangular window at the front of the chalet. Set against the back wall of the house, a new mezzanine level replaces the old bedroom. The mezzanine is bounded by sturdy netting so that the trees remain visible from the cozy loft bed.

The architects clad the entire interior in textural OSB panels, a low-cost solution that also adds an extra layer of insulation. Outside, they added larch cladding to the rear of the building, and carefully restored the aluminum-framed glass facade. The green-painted front door now leads out to a new split-level terrace—complete with a slide—that connects the cabin with the thick mountain forest on its doorstep. When the weather is warm enough, this spacious deck provides an area for outdoor dining and relaxation, as well as a children's play area beneath the age-old trees.

This diamond-shaped vacation cabin floats on stilts above an area of bogland in Estonia's Rapla County. Designed by b210, an architecture studio based in Tallinn, Estonia, the hideaway has a triangular terrace and a staggered roof composed of steps and platforms, culminating in a lookout point at the top. The compact abode was designed to immerse visitors in the tranquility of this wild site, which is part of the Maidla Nature Resort.

With just one room inside, with space for two to sleep, the cabin's main feature is its V-shaped window that projects out through the foliage into the bog. Trees on either side of the window create a feeling of refuge and allow the eye to roam outward across the unspoiled wilderness. Just inside the tip of the spear-like window is a wood-burning stove; at the other side of the cabin, a small bathroom is tucked behind a partition wall. A sofa (which doubles as a child's futon) sits opposite the wood-burning stove at the foot of the bed, where a curtain can be drawn to separate the two zones.

The exterior of the house is clad in rich-hued thermo-treated ash, making it a discreet addition to the landscape. The stilts beneath reach a depth of 23 feet (7 meters) below ground, ensuring a solid foundation despite the boggy terrain. In the spring, the entire area becomes flooded by a nearby river, so the house can only be reached by an elevated boardwalk or by canoe, for those who wish to take to the water.

Owners Kjartan and Sally Aano dreamed up Woodnest, two small but perfectly formed vacation retreats in the Odda municipality of Norway. Suspended 20 feet (6 meters) above the forest floor, each timber tree house hovers dramatically over a steep hillside that slopes down to the vast Hardangerfjord.

Realized by Norwegian practice Helen & Hard, each 161-square-foot (15-square-meter) house is reached using a bridge, via a winding footpath that leads up through the woods. A timber-lined interior provides space for up to four—as well as a bathroom, kitchen, and living space—all of which are organized around the trunk of a living tree.

The construction of the tree houses draws on Norwegian architectural traditions, though the architects experimented with new ways of working with wood. A steel collar fastens each house to the tree with minimal harm to the trunk, which in turn gives support to the structure. The exteriors of the tiny dwellings are clad in untreated timber shingles that form a protective shell and will weather over time to blend in with the forest.

Sitting quietly up in the treetops, looking out at the spectacular setting, Woodnest has an ingenious design that encourages visitors to notice the smallest details of their natural surroundings—whether that's the grain of the wood that fills the space, the daily rhythm of the forest, or the light changing over the fjord below.

Hidden in a pine forest, close to a sprawling lake in China's Jiangxi province, ZJJZ's The Mushroom is a 538-square-foot (50-square-meter) guesthouse built from concrete, wood, and steel. The client, hotel company Tree Wow, wanted to help visitors escape the ordinary, so the Shanghai-based studio designed a distinctive cone-shaped roof, which lends the house a quirky, fairy-tale quality.

ZJJZ opted to elevate the house on stilts to reduce construction impact. The architects chose to clad the building's exterior in granolithic concrete and to cover the roof with pine shingles because both materials respond to the elements and evolve over time, helping the house to take on the colors of the landscape.

The round portion of the architecture is dedicated to a semicircular, timber-lined bedroom, where a panoramic ribbon window offers tree-framed views in every direction. A simple rectangular volume connects the bedroom to the home's entrance, while also comprising built-in storage and a compact bathroom. A slender, horizontal window rests above the bath, letting the daylight in yet shielding the space from view. A round skylight has been integrated into the ceiling. Between the bedroom and bathroom, a small staircase ascends to a loft area that provides a cozy space for children to sleep, tucked up under the conical roof and soothed by the sounds of the forest.

Measuring just 409-square-feet (38-square-meters), this tiny home in Japan's Nagano prefecture was crafted by hand from clay and wood using traditional building techniques. It was designed by nearby firm Tono Mirai Architects, which worked with regional craftsmen to fulfill the client's request for a beautiful, unusual forest dwelling that coexists happily with its surroundings.

The architects conceived the building's organic shape to ensure it looked at home in its woodland setting. An intricate timber structure forms the framework of the house, which is covered externally with a protective sheath of wooden tiles that extends to the tip of the peaked overhang, with the eaves made of Hanegi. Inside, soft curved earthen walls wrap around a bathroom, kitchen, and living area on the ground floor, and a loft space above. Furniture has been kept down to essentials, to avoid detracting from the handcrafted simplicity of the structure and woodland scenery. A small stove helps to keep the compact space warm in cold weather, and clever built-in solutions, such as a raised dining area with storage beneath, allow the house to remain free of clutter.

Through the use of age-old building techniques and traditional materials, the home manages to surpass modern energy standards, more than satisfying Japan's current requirements. The passive building harnesses the natural properties of its clay walls to store heat and control humidity. A large aperture at the front admits sunlight and helps to make the most of the green and peaceful forest setting, strengthening the connection between this primordial-looking home and its environment.

This prefabricated, carbon-neutral house occupies a leafy corner of a Dutch forest. Amsterdam-based architecture firm Woonpioniers codesigned it with the homeowners, who are leasing a plot of land in this wooded area near Barchem, Gelderland. The modular timber-and-glass building is intelligently designed to leave no trace once removed. It rests on a foundation of concrete beams and pier blocks that can be extricated easily from the sandy soil.

The house itself is made of prefabricated timber panels, which minimized the environmental impact of the construction process. Stained larch has been used for the exterior, while inside the apex roof, spruce cladding curves down to meet the walls. This design feature helps to distribute the structural load, so internal supports can be kept to a minimum. The result is an airy and spacious interior, where light floods in through the glass facade and permeates the entire house.

A living and dining area can be found just inside the home's entrance, set against the backdrop of uninterrupted greenery visible through the cabin's apex window. Beyond this, small vestibules create additional spaces, separating the living area from the bedrooms and enclosing the different portions of the building, making them easier to heat. Renewable energy sources further increase the structure's sustainability. Solar energy is harvested from panels on a nearby building, because the house's forest site is shady. The underfloor heating system draws power from an air-to-water pump, and the thermal mass of the ground beneath helps to regulate internal temperatures, ensuring comfort throughout the seasons.

This German home is made up of five overlapping boxes, which have been arranged around the pines on a woodland plot. Berlin and Mexico City–based architecture studio Zeller & Moye conceived the lakeside abode, which is in a small forest clearing close to the village of Klein Köris in Dahme-Spreewald.

The home features a raised design chosen to protect the forest floor, while its staggered formation preserves the trees around it. The series of elevated cubes enclose separate spaces devoted to living, sleeping, and working, with the central box providing an open-plan area at the heart of the house. The succession of compact outdoor niches surrounding the perimeter of the building are an added benefit of the fragmented floor plan. Some of these alcoves are sheltered from the wind or hidden from sight; others are idyllic suntraps. All of them help to enhance the home's connection to its surroundings by offering additional outlooks and incentivizing inhabitants to enjoy time outside among the trees.

The exterior of the house is clad in boards made from locally sourced spruce, and the inside was constructed using modular wooden building blocks and solid-wood slabs. Even the insulation is made of wood-based fiber. Picture windows punctuate the rooms, allowing natural light to bounce around the pale-wood spaces. The windows mimic landscape paintings, with swaths of greenery and slender tree trunks filling their frames.

Two mature trees grow up through an outdoor living area in this home in the Mexican city of Guadalajara. Working closely with local architect Javier Rosales Iriondo, Argentinian firm la base studio came up with the concept in response to the temperate climate and the plot's existing vegetation, which the architects were keen to preserve.

At ground level, a covered L-shaped terrace serves as a sheltered outdoor living-dining area in close proximity to the kitchen. Separating this terrace from the adjacent building is a line of ferns, which envelop the bases of the two trees. Above this, a gallery walkway lined with terracotta tiles wraps around the trunks. The walkway, which provides access to the bedrooms on the upper level, offers views of the surrounding trees in one direction and the garden in the other.

The house is made up of three volumes, separated by patio areas, private courtyards, and pockets of green, which offer ample space to introduce more plantings and emphasize the home's indoor-outdoor feel. The interior palette combines raw concrete with rich-hued tropical ipe wood, bringing warmth and texture in abundance. The lead architects on the project, Alejandro Sticotti and Nicolas Tovo, designed and fabricated custom fixtures in metal and wood, as well as much of the furniture. Perhaps the most inviting space is the ground-floor main bedroom, which leads out to the pool area. Here, stone terraces have been created around the garden's trees, providing a leafy oasis in the middle of the city.

CHAMELEON VILLA
2017 | Buwit, Bali

Designed by Bali-based architecture firm Word of Mouth House, this Balinese home emerges from the rainforest like a jagged rock formation covered in trailing greenery. Built into the contours of a lush valley in Buwit, close to the island's southern beaches, the two-story house has a poolside terrace overlooking the Jeh Poh river below. The moniker Chameleon Villa was inspired by the home's ability to simultaneously emerge from and disappear into the surrounding landscape.

With its clean, contemporary form crafted from a considered combination of locally sourced materials, the villa has a distinctly organic quality, as well as a moderate carbon footprint. The stacked rectangular volumes are positioned at angles to help the building integrate into the hillside; green roofs blanketed in tumbling cascades of vegetation soften the edges of the impressive structure and serve as additional camouflage. A passive cooling method, solar panels, water recycling, and a rainwater collection system add to the home's green credentials.

In the floor plan, the architect Valentina Audrito opted to screen or enclose the more private spaces within the house—such as the bedrooms, office, gym, and media room—while the communal areas are opened up to the elements on three sides. Interiors offer a Tropical Modern take on luxury: think platform beds, sunken baths, midcentury-inspired furniture, and rattan accents, set against a backdrop of cool concrete and rich-hued timber. Pops of hothouse color can be seen throughout, perfectly complementing the verdant rainforest that's visible from almost every corner.

With capuchin monkeys inhabiting the trees around the dwelling, this property is known as the Monkey House. Offering an eco-friendly escape for those seeking the solitude of the Brazilian rainforest, the house is located close to the coastal town of Paraty, in an area of second-growth forest that covers a former banana plantation. The architect, São Paulo–based Marko Brajovic, has turned the land into a nature reserve, building additional eco-conscious homes on the property, which is peppered with natural pools and hiking trails.

The A-frame cabin, located in Brazil's ecological sanctuary Aldeia Rizoma, is surrounded by native juçara palms, which inspired the ingenious design. The garapeira wood Monkey House has a footprint of just 16½ × 19½ feet (5 × 6 meters); its stilts mimic the roots of the juçara palm, which spread out from the tree's base to anchor its tall and slender trunk to the ground. As such, the house is elevated on a raised platform, with strong, slim concrete stilts that adapt the platform to the uneven terrain. The timber-frame building tapers to form a pointed roof, clad in Galvalume metal panels, which stretches up into the forest canopy.

For the architecture and interiors, Brajovic looked to the climate-responsive homes of the indigenous Guaraní community. He used native hardwoods and woven bamboo throughout the passively cooled house, which contains a kitchen, living area, bedroom, bathroom, and top-floor observatory that offers space for yoga and meditation among the trees.

Reached via a rope bridge suspended through a dry tropical forest, this contemporary Costa Rican jungle hideaway has an air of adventure. In collaboration with interior designer Pauline Steenkamer, local design studio VIDA drew from the regional architectural vernacular to create the thatched pavilion, which is high up in the hills on the Pacific coast.

The 59 foot (18 meter) suspension bridge enabled the architects to provide access to the remote plot without disrupting the surrounding vegetation—a primary concern throughout the project. Despite the thick rainforest that covers the entire site, only two trees needed to be removed during the construction of the building, which cantilevers over the hillside and is mostly open to the elements.

Crafted from solid concrete with timber posts and accents, the white-walled home features a modest entrance that leads visitors through a small enclosed portion and into a spacious, airy terrace where a kitchen and dining area drops down to meet outdoor seating. Beyond this is an infinity pool that floats above the forest, set against a backdrop of ocean views and shaded by the leafy jungle canopy.

A weatherproof thatched roof—the home's most characteristic feature—extends out to form a rustic, timber-framed canopy that feels perfectly at one with the jungle setting. Beneath it, the design is robust yet inviting, with coralina stone floors, a chunky timber dining table, and a generous sofa for outdoor lounging. Ceiling fans hang overhead, helping to keep the air circulating through the house, while statement lighting in woven designs casts atmospheric shadows after the sun goes down.

TALA TREEHOUSE VILLA
2017 | Tala, India

Surrounded by 160 acres (65 hectares) of tropical forest, this tree house villa occupies an idyllic hilltop spot in Tala, a small town in the Raigad district of Maharashtra state, which is close to India's west coast. Dutch-Indian firm Architecture Brio designed the villa as part of purpose-built eco-resort Forest Hills.

Perched on the edge of a steep escarpment, the luxurious tree house is supported by two staggered platforms that have been constructed around the woodland growing on the hillside. Its spacious, curved volumes are enclosed by wraparound glass walls and topped with a pointed thatched roof. Wide, timber-framed doors lead out to a generous raised deck with incredible panoramic views over the Khajaniwadi river estuary, which meanders out to the Arabian Sea.

The deceptively spacious two-story structure is equipped with two double beds, a loft bed for children, two bathrooms, a living area, a pantry, and an outdoor dining area.

For privacy, beds are surrounded by gauzy white linen curtains, which—when combined with pale, polished stone floors and white partition walls—create a pristine backdrop that contrasts beautifully with the home's dark-wood structure and interior details.

Rather than breaking up the floor plan with enclosed rooms, the architects opted to zone the space with subtle gestures, allowing the full panorama to be visible through the building's curved glass walls. One highlight is an outdoor bathroom, where the trunk of a garuga fruit tree pierces the floor and walls. Here, guests can bathe beneath its leafy canopy and soak up the sights and sounds of the rainforest.

A prototype positioned on the edge of a Costa Rican rainforest, this prefabricated, zero-carbon house in Ojochal responds to the surrounding environment through site-specific positioning and passive climate control. A-01 used natural ventilation and solar shading to keep the house comfortable despite the warm and humid weather conditions in the Puntarenas province, on the country's South Pacific coast. Based in Costa Rica and the Netherlands, the interdisciplinary studio is on a mission to push the boundaries of sustainable construction.

To achieve their aim, the architects organized the building's layout around a central service unit, which contains the bathrooms, kitchen, and laundry area. This meant that the rest of the spaces could remain completely open, with temperature, light, and ventilation controlled by the motorized facade made up of louvered blinds. The slant of the facade also reduces direct sunlight and precipitation, while an elevated steel foundation ensures minimal contact with the land.

One of the added bonuses of the building's pioneering design is that the surrounding landscape is visible from almost every point in the house, allowing inhabitants to feel immersed in the tropical forest that encircles it. The wooden blinds can be opened or closed individually to adjust the views or increase privacy. This versatility allows much of the interior to be converted into a single open-air space and encourages interplay between the building and its environment. Upstairs, bedrooms are partitioned by sliding glass doors and "curtain walls" for unobstructed sight lines, while all around the home's perimeter the blinds and dense vegetation cast dappled layers of light and shade across the elegant timber floors.

SANDIBE OKAVANGO SAFARI LODGE
2016 | Okavango Delta, Botswana

This luxury eco-lodge in Botswana features a curved exterior covered with shingles that mimic the protective scales of the native pangolin. Located in the heart of the vast Okavango Delta, in the northwest of the country, Sandibe Okavango Safari Lodge was designed by South African practice Nicholas Plewman Architects, in collaboration with studio Michaelis Boyd.

The lodge is built on part of a UNESCO World Heritage site, which meant the project needed to adhere to strict criteria. To meet government guidelines, all materials had to be biodegradable, and 70 percent of energy consumption had to come from sustainable sources, in this case, largely solar power. To meet these requirements, the boutique hotel is constructed almost entirely out of wood, with its exterior of cedar shingles and beams made from glulam South African pine. The building is raised up on timber stilts to limit its physical impact on the land and features latticed panels made from sustainably sourced eucalyptus.

Winding through the trees dotted across the site, the lodge combines eco-friendly construction with high-end hospitality. Trees that could not be avoided have been incorporated into the design, their gnarled trunks stretching up through floors and ceilings, or woven into the latticed panels. Around them, a luxurious interior unfolds, fusing rustic materials with five-star comfort. Testament to the project's successful integration, lions, leopards, hippos, and elephants continue to frequent the site, with the hotel's elevated, tree-fringed interior forming the perfect viewing platform for wildlife.

Sited among tall oaks and coastal pines, this Danish home stands alone in a meadow on the west coast of Sjælland. Expansive northerly views create a sense of freedom and openness, while the thicket of trees surrounding the plot contributes to an underlying ambience of restfulness and protection. Designed by Copenhagen-based Jan Henrik Jansen Arkitekter, in collaboration with Australian architect Marshall Blecher, it serves as a peaceful second home on the waterfront for its city-dwelling owners.

A monolithic structure constructed from Italian travertine, the sculptural house crouches low on its grassy plot, accentuating the line of trees to the rear. At its center is a glass-walled living space with a raised ceiling and clerestory windows that allow additional light to flow down into the timber-lined interior. To one side is a bedroom with views over the sea to the neighboring island of Sejerø, while at the other end of the building, a covered outdoor dining area leads off the kitchen. Joinery, built-in furniture, window frames, and ceilings have been crafted from honey-colored oiled oak, creating a mellow backdrop for a collection of midcentury furniture.

Tucked behind the main living space is a travertine-walled terrace, which separates the home's entrance from its oak-paneled front gates. This versatile area is made up of a series of sheltered spaces set between the hawthorn trees that spring up through the decked floor. Designed for family gatherings as well as quiet contemplation, the terrace contains a tranquil reflection pool and provides refuge from the coastal winds.

[3] BUILT TO BECOME THE FOREST

From a modest microhome hidden in a Hungarian woodland to a monolithic jungle dwelling that juts out of a Brazilian mountainside, the houses that make up this chapter push the boundaries of what's possible in forest living. For these projects, located on remote sites and inhospitable terrain, the architects embraced the wildness of the landscape and rose to the many challenges it presented. The resulting homes provide complete immersion in nature, as well as a modus operandi for building respectfully in unspoiled surrounds.

One example is Frankie Pappas's House of the Big Arch: an off-grid abode composed of narrow buildings, bridges, and courtyards that weave, almost unseen, through a nature reserve in South Africa's Waterberg Mountains. Exemplary in its approach, the design responded to its owners' desire for a home that disappears into the landscape, and one that offers animals, plants, and humans equal opportunity to find shelter. Other creative designs that become one with the wild include a sunken, underground structure concealed beneath a hillside in Mexico, and a tiny Finnish cabin set on a single slender column surrounded by towering pines.

It's evident, when poring over these pioneering projects, that nature provides an unending playbook of design strategies and motifs from which architects can draw inspiration. The visual language of these varied landscapes is transmitted through the homes that inhabit them like an echo, from asymmetric roofs that align with the treetops to angular buildings that mirror the rugged outlines of their rocky plots. These projects don't attempt to tame the land; instead, they strike a balance between creating a place of refuge and embracing the raw, untainted beauty of the surrounding environment.

This delicate equipoise between architecture and the natural world has a direct effect on day-to-day life in these extraordinary homes. Whether it's the subtle interplay between enclosed and exposed spaces, an interior experience that simulates walking through the trees, or a facade that takes on the colors of the forest, the end result is a therapeutic dissolution of the divide between humankind and nature.

CASA NA CANIÇADA

2021 | Vieira do Minho, Portugal

This monastic concrete house is nestled in a forest, close to the Caniçada Dam in Vieira do Minho, a rural municipality in northern Portugal. The three-story family home was built on the site of a preexisting property, which was demolished in favor of a better quality, more contemporary design. Local architecture studio Carvalho Araújo designed the new clean-lined, glass-and-concrete structure to be an unobtrusive addition to the woodland setting.

In order to ensure minimal disruption to the surrounding vegetation, the size and shape of the old building informed the proportions of the new one. The sloping plot means that part of the lower level is sunk into the leafy hillside, while on the ground level, floor-to-ceiling glass windows and sliding doors open the minimalist living area up to the forest. One of these apertures forms the home's impressive entrance, accessed by a winding path of concrete steps; the other frames a view of the reservoir below.

The exterior material palette extends inside the house, where walls, floors, and ceilings are clad in lustrous polished concrete. The top floor contains four bedrooms enclosed by glass partitions lined with wraparound curtains for privacy. Here, the slant of the gabled roof helps to create a subtle sense of intimacy, which offsets the striking austerity of this unconventional country home.

A timber-frame home that mimics the shape of a branch, House in the Forest was created with peace and solitude in mind. The mountain retreat is located in Hokkaido, Japan, close to the busy ski slopes of Niseko, which is a global destination for those in search of snow. Sited within 7 acres (3 hectares) of secluded, unspoiled forest, the single-story residence was designed as an escape from the ever-increasing tourist bustle of the surrounding area.

To enhance the feeling of seclusion, the house is tucked into the corner of a large clearing that's encircled by tall pine trees. It can only be reached via a small rural road and is hidden from view by the undulating mountainous terrain.

To make moving between rooms feel like walking through the forest, Tokyo-based Florian Busch Architects gave the building a raised design that branches out horizontally.

At the end of each branch is a glass aperture; this makes the home's extremities feel more exposed and, by comparison, intensifies the protective feel of its timber-lined central spaces. The finished project owes its success to a process of probing, and responding to, the unique topography of this mountain site. This is a place where the owners, a large family that fell in love with the natural beauty of the region, can enjoy time together and separately, while feeling at one with the forest.

For this linear, cedar-clad Canadian hideaway, architecture studio MRDK drew inspiration from cabins in the Norwegian mountains. Japanese design also inspired the vacation home's refreshing and tactile take on minimalism. The studio designed Hinterhouse for hotel concept Hinter. Eco-conscious in its company ethos—Hinter plants ten trees for every booking made.

The hideaway is constructed almost entirely from sustainably forested native wood. White cedar covers the boxy exterior, which features large sliding shutters that can conceal and reveal the house and the views. When the shutters are open, the woodland becomes one with the interior; when closed, the dwelling transforms into a cozy and cocooning haven, complete with a crackling wood-burning stove.

White-oiled planks of red pine and dark-stained Douglas fir plywood clad walls and ceilings inside; a poured concrete floor completes the textural material palette. Fixtures and furniture are purposely understated, and clever custom solutions—such as a multipurpose kitchen island and built-in under-bed storage—help to save space and maintain the home's streamlined aesthetic. The only real color comes from the vibrant green of the trees that are visible from every one of the structure's generous windows.

Designed with a focus on well-being, the house has its own sauna with full-height apertures that look out to the forest. In this space, as in the main residence, visitors are encouraged to slow down, reconnect with nature, and immerse themselves in mountain living.

Built in the shape of a perfect circle, this timber house is in a forest clearing in Warsaw West county in Poland. Located in the village of Izabelin, the rural retreat is just a short drive from the county's capital city but has the UNESCO site and biosphere reserve Kampinos National Park at its doorstep. Warsaw and Kraków-based architecture studio Mobius Architekci designed the house for an art lover and collector, who asked for the architecture to feature gallery-like spaces that would provide a backdrop to his collection and bring the beauty of the forest inside.

In response to this brief, the studio incorporated soaring white-walled spaces of impressive proportions, as well as double-height windows that fill the house with light. More intimate rooms balance the grand scale of the larger volumes in the two-story living quarters, which are positioned around one side of the circle. On the other side is a covered terrace with a grass roof, leaving an open courtyard garden at its center.

Pine trees spring up through and beside the terrace, maintaining a strong connection between the forest and the house, which is constructed from reinforced concrete and clad in okoume wood panels. Circular motifs can be found in and around the building, accentuating its playful geometric quality. The shapes also nod to architect and founder Przemek Olczyk's original inspiration for the design: he imagined the house as a massive piece of tree trunk, hewn and carved into an encircling woodland shelter.

Concealed in the rainforest canopy near Guarujá, a city on the São Paulo coast, this statuesque concrete home was created by Brazilian design firm Studio MK27. The scale of the project was determined by the natural clearing in which it sits, allowing the surrounding forest to dictate its footprint. Designed to look like an extension of the undulating coastline, the house emerges from the stepped clearing to become a part of the mass of tropical vegetation that covers the hillside.

In order to make the most of the sea views and natural light, the architects placed the home's main living spaces and pool area on the rooftop of the building. Six bedrooms are nestled beneath, inside the main body of the board-marked-concrete house. A large wooden deck covers the indoor and outdoor spaces on the rooftop, where a glass-walled, flat-roofed structure shelters the living and dining

areas with its generous overhang. A glazed balcony surrounds the swimming pool and fire pit to the front, ensuring an uninterrupted sight line over the treetops to the Atlantic Ocean. A smaller terrace can be found at the back of the house—complete with a sauna and sunken hot tub—where the decking traces the rocky contours of the hillside.

To optimize cross ventilation, the walls of the interior living quarters retract completely, turning the space into a pergola-like structure that is cooled by the coastal breeze. Retracting the walls also serves to heighten inhabitants' immersion in the natural landscape. The home's interior scheme was conceived to further enhance this sense of connection, with walls of exposed concrete and timber, and furnishings chosen for their organic, unfussy feel.

This carbon-colored seasonal retreat juts out of the forest over Christina Lake in southern British Columbia, Canada. Working in association with Miller Mottola Calabro, American studio Bohlin Cywinski Jackson designed the cabin as a summer escape for an artist and her family. Its plot is the highest point on the lake's shore, heightening the visual impact of the home's cantilevered design by providing a breathtaking outlook across the lake to the tree-covered peaks beyond. The project adds to the studio's portfolio of contemporary residences specifically built to foster a close connection with awe-inspiring natural surroundings.

Dark-stained Western red cedar covers the exterior of the wedge-shaped structure, which mirrors the slope of the rocky outcrop on which it sits. A forest of towering conifers surrounds the house on three sides, adding to its secluded feel. On one side is a wood trellis supported on slender steel columns that mirror the tree trunks while a sheltered terrace hovers over the lake at the front of the house. By opening up a portion of the home's facade along one side of this terrace, the architects brought the southern curve of the lake into view, creating a spectacular vista.

Inside, the home combines traditional hallmarks of cabin architecture—such as timber-beamed ceilings in the open kitchen, cozy loft bedrooms, a wood-burning stove, and windows to the wild—with airy rooms and streamlined interior architecture. A relaxed, light-filled kitchen with an indoor-outdoor feel combines a wall of birch plywood cabinetry with a U-shaped island and convivial bar seating. It's a perfect place for the family to gather after a day out on the lake or hiking in the forest.

Set on a single steel column and flanked by soaring pines in Finland's Salamajärvi National Park, this black-painted cabin is a contemporary take on traditional wooden huts found in Lapland. The indigenous Sami people elevated the huts to keep food and other provisions safe from wild animals. Studio Puisto, a practice based in Helsinki, reinterpreted the age-old design to create a prototype for cabins in a new resort in Kivijärvi, honoring the region's Sami heritage while ensuring minimal disruption to the land.

Raising the tiny retreat up into the air was also a way to help resort visitors detach from their day-to-day concerns and immerse themselves in the wildness of the park. Studio Puisto strategically placed the cabin to avoid cutting down trees, so the house feels completely shielded by the woods. The supporting column is set into a foundation beneath the ground so that, in time, the forest floor can reclaim the terrain under the house.

A tree-lined path leads to the staircase up to the home's entrance. When visitors step inside, the dark-stained pine exterior gives way to a light, wood-paneled interior that boasts all the comforts of a modern hotel. Clever interior layout keeps walls and ceiling surfaces free of visual clutter. A kitchenette, bathroom, and all technical necessities are in a central core. The design ensures that the main focus is the view through an apex window at the foot of the bed, enhancing the experience of sleeping among the pines.

LITTLE HOUSE / BIG SHED

2021 | Whidbey Island, WA, USA

Owned and designed by architect David Van Galen, this Pacific Northwest retreat is in an area of established second-growth woodland on Whidbey Island in Puget Sound. Van Galen and his wife discovered the 5 acre (2 hectare) property during a winter walk through this former logging site, which is now home to a thriving forest of red alders and towering Douglas firs.

After purchasing the land, the Seattle-based architect and painter set about designing the vacation home and adjacent studio on an elevated platform at the edge of a ravine. He decided to break the house up into two separate structures to protect a fir tree growing at the center of the plot, which is reached by a gravel drive that traces an old tractor path. Covering both facades, untreated Corten steel panels have been left to rust naturally, turning a mottled brown that blends in harmoniously with the woodland.

A large deck connects the two buildings, both of which are punctuated by expansive windows and topped with sloping roofs that stretch up toward the trees. Uncomplicated floor plans define both building's light-filled interiors, with a kitchen, dining room, living area, bedroom, and bathroom in the main residence and a single room in the studio that doubles as a guest quarters. Throughout construction, Van Galen avoided disturbing the surrounding woodland as much as possible, and he has since replenished impacted areas with native vegetation, such as salal shrubs, vine maples, and ferns.

ROMA HOUSE
2020 | Moscow, Russia

Built in a thicket of centuries-old pine trees, not far from Moscow, this staggering dwelling seems much larger than its 2,260-square-foot (210-square-meter) floor plan and serves as a much-needed hideout from the bustle of the city. Russian studio buro511 came up with the design to fulfill its client's wish for a house that combined the feel of a luxurious apartment with that of a back-to-basics forest retreat.

The result is a highly personal, idiosyncratic home that expresses a variety of design languages adapted to the owner and their changing and conflicting desires. Despite the convoluted route to completion, the house achieves everything it set out to do with its arresting steel, glass, and timber exterior, as well as its polished interior scheme. At its center is a double-height living space with a huge

Crittall-inspired window, which brings penthouse style to the heart of the forest. Camouflaged against the back wall is an all-black kitchen, where an island extends fluidly into a long dining table. Behind this volume, single-story, timber-screened wings extend outward, containing the bathrooms and guest bedrooms.

The material palette combines luxurious finishes with an abundance of texture, from the walnut veneer washbasins to the rough-hewn Turkish stone fireplace. Custom joinery emphasizes the high-end aesthetic, while concrete wall panels create a Brutalist atmosphere. Relaxed furnishings, such as the low-slung sectional sofa that fills the living space, ensure that the overriding atmosphere is one of uncompromising comfort.

This remote escape in a forest in Hungary's Alpokalja region is raised on stilts to have the lowest possible impact on the land. Designed by Budapest studio Béres Architects, the 431-square-foot (40-square-meter) cabin offers all the necessary comforts of home within the confines of a compact space. The owner of the three-room timber house, Attila Hideg, asked the architects for a design that he could build singlehandedly. The residence's angular shape creates extra height and depth, while the stilted base negates the need for an excavated foundation, thus protecting the roots of the hundred-year-old trees that encircle the house.

Inside, pale wooden planks line the walls and ceiling of the main living and dining space, which is fitted with a slim kitchenette and features a picture window. Pocket doors lead to a tiny bathroom that acts as an antechamber to the bedroom beyond. For simplicity, a bank of cabinetry extends the full length of the house—from the kitchen units all the way to the bedroom, encompassing the bathroom vanity area and providing storage for clothes.

The house is positioned to turn its back on the few neighbors that are dotted along the dead-end access road; the front benefits from uninterrupted forest views. All energy for heating and hot water is electric, while the cozy timber-lined interior is well insulated which further lowers the energy consumption of the property. The orientation of the windows allows for maximum ventilation, capitalizing on the forest's microclimate and keeping the house cool throughout the warm months.

Designed as a direct response to the natural beauty of its coastal setting, this Australian vacation home perches on a ridge within an area of bushland in Djiringanj country, New South Wales. The angular structure, which occupies the former site of an old cottage, is a discreet addition to the secluded valley adjacent to Tathra Beach.

Sydney, Australia–based architecture firm Welsh + Major chose brick as the main building material, to help the house blend in with the rocky headland. The use of this robust material is also a protective measure that's intended to safeguard the building in the event of a bushfire. For the building's form, the architects mirrored the landscape: the brick is corbeled—a technique that allows the walls to jut outward at an angle—projecting the upper floor toward the tree canopy, while embedding the building into the steep slope of the valley.

Created as a tranquil woodland sanctuary for its owners, the residence is largely hidden from the beach, due to the scrubby headland and abundance of trees. Despite the elevated setting and incredible coastal views, Welsh + Major decided not to incorporate an outdoor deck because of the home's wild location, which is exposed to the elements. Instead, the home's upper floor offers an enclosed and protected area to take in the views of the bush, beach, and sea. Outside, tucked between the house and the surrounding trees, a small clearing to one side of the structure provides a sheltered spot to sit outside and admire the vista.

Flanked by ancient trees on a sloping site in Ponte da Barca in northern Portugal, this concrete-and-glass home is high above the ground, level with the treetops. It was built for an artist by Portuguese firm Marques Franco Arquitectos, whose aim was to create an unobtrusive home that became one with the tree canopy, allowing the landscape to "invade" the house.

To realize this goal, the architects designed the residence with floor-to-ceiling glazing on all sides, and sliding doors that open to fuse the interior with the wide balcony encircling the building. Instead of choosing which aspects of the surroundings to highlight and which to conceal, the firm preferred to provide views in all directions, thus allowing the eye to roam the landscape freely. The same material palette was applied to both the exterior and interior of the house to provide continuity, with concrete chosen for its ability to take on the colors of the foliage over time, helping the facade to blend in with the surrounding oak and chestnut trees.

Support pillars for the flat roof are dotted inside and outside of the home's internal perimeter, further dissolving the line between the house and the forest. Interior divides have been kept to a minimum, with multipurpose furniture units used to partition most of the rooms, apart from the bathrooms, which are fully enclosed. Neutral hues feature throughout the interior, ensuring the olive, oak, and chestnut trees that surround the building bring the spaces to life with their contrasting tones and textures, which evolve constantly throughout the seasons.

When the clients first approached architecture firm Frankie Pappas about designing this off-grid home in South Africa's Waterberg Mountains, the brief was simple: to create a house within the tree canopy without cutting down a single tree. The reality of achieving this feat was a little more complicated, so the Johannesburg-based firm set to work devising a series of buildings, bridges, arches, and raised courtyards that weave through the trees to form a single interconnected dwelling.

The team at Frankie Pappas designed the buildings to be just 11 feet (3.3 meters) wide, as a way to conceal the house within the bushveld. The layout of the trees and the topography of the sandstone cliff dictated the design and construction of the slender structures. Their flat roofs are covered in native vegetation, and their walls have curved sections to accommodate tree trunks.

At the home's center is its kitchen and dining space; the latter is flanked by glass doors that invite the riverine forest inside. A compact living space opens onto a small natural courtyard; this creates a pocket of high-pressure air that pushes cool air from outside back into the house. The highly eco-friendly house features sustainable timber throughout. Rainwater from the roofs is collected and filtered; electricity is generated by 172-square-feet (16-square-meters) of solar panels; and the architecture works with the environment to create a shady, ventilated, and acclimatized space with minimal energy demands.

THE HILL IN FRONT OF THE GLEN

2021 | Morelia, Mexico

With the sweeping lines of its curved roof barely visible above the ground, this sunken home in the Mexican state of Michoacán is a contextually sensitive addition to its forest setting. From above, the low-lying, grass-covered house becomes one with the hilly landscape; inside, a huge arched window frames the edge of a tree-lined ravine.

The project is by HW Studio Arquitectos, which is based in nearby Morelia. The architects came up with the vaulted concrete design as a structural solution, enabling them to build a significant portion of the house below ground level. A long, concrete-walled walkway leads up to the entrance, which is hidden from view by a tall pine tree that is rooted squarely in the center of the path.

To create a quiet moment for contemplation in the presence of the old tree, the architects deliberately chose to make the corridor just wide enough for a single person to walk through comfortably. One of the walls along the walkway bends to accommodate the trunk, providing space to pass around it.

Past the heavy steel front door, inside the house a corridor divides the kitchen, dining area, and living space from the home's three bedrooms. Interiors of wood, concrete, and steel echo the ruggedness of the mountain location, while the curved ceiling is designed to mimic the act of enveloping oneself in a blanket, which is part of the architects' plan to make a house like a protective forest bower.

HOUSE ON THE CAUTÍN RIVER
2020 | Malalcahuello, Chile

When Santiago-based studio Iragüen Viñuela Arquitectos was enlisted to design a vacation home in the Chilean Andes, its first task was to decide how best to make use of an existing steel-and-wood foundation on the site, which was the result of a failed construction attempt by a previous contractor. Iragüen Viñuela recycled it, using it to define the floor plan and position of the new project.

The completed house is in a tree-lined clearing in Araucanía, close to the popular ski resort of Corralco. An unpretentious structure clad in sun-bleached timber with a gabled roof, it offers space for twelve to sleep and features a spacious communal area with large windows on both sides. The layout capitalizes on the natural beauty of the plot; a corridor leads to a view of the Cautín river, while the communal area opens to both north and south so that sun can flood in throughout the day. Black wood interiors provide a striking contrast to the snow-covered surroundings in winter, as well as the vivid greenery of spring and summer.

To enhance the home's connection to its forest setting, the studio designed a series of platforms that branch out from the house, bypassing existing trees and encouraging inhabitants to wander out to different areas on the plot. These elevated walkways make the outdoors more accessible in heavy snow and connect to a long deck that culminates in a wooden swimming pool, and a second deck under huge trees that leads to a hot tub by the river.

An imposing home with a surprisingly small footprint, this Russian forest dwelling was designed to take up as little of the land as possible while providing enough space for multiple families to visit together in comfort. Instead of extending out horizontally, Saint Petersburg practice Horomystudio opted to build upward, creating a monolithic six-story residence with an angular timber exterior.

The building's ambitious narrow plan left the surrounding woodland intact, preserving a line of trees around the house that enhances its outlook. A small portion of the home has been built into the hillside; the rest sits on an elevated foundation that straddles an access road beneath the property. Dark-stained wood encases the faceted exterior, with charcoal-colored cladding on the rear section of the house and a rich brown timber covering the front facade. Windows of varying sizes punctuate the walls in an irregular formation chosen to offer the best views of the wooded landscape, which stretches as far as the eye can see.

Towering high above the snow-covered ground, the impressive structure culminates in a stepped, pointed roof design that echoes the outline of the coniferous forest behind. Inside, the home is streamlined and understated, with pale-wood floors and neutral walls forming a pleasing contrast with the dark exterior. Trees fill the frames of the picture windows, and a communal living area provides space for families to relax and dine together, surrounded on all sides by the majestic beauty of the Russian forest.

PRISM HOUSE + TERRACE ROOM

2019 | Conguillío National Park, Chile

Internationally acclaimed Chilean architect Smiljan Radić designed this striking mountain home, which is composed of two triangular volumes linked by an elevated deck made of blackened Oregon pine. The house is situated on a wooded slope in the Andes, close to the Llaima volcano within Conguillío National Park. Its deck is sheltered by a tall tree that grows up through the stepped surface, which spans the length of the 19,810-square-foot (1,840-square-meter) property.

Framed by the trees above, the angular volumes are an arresting sight, with their pointed black corrugated-metal roofs echoing the shapes of the nearby peaks. The Prism House is an attempt to re-create that of its namesake by Kazuo Shinohara, which was built in Japan, close

to Mount Fuji, in the 1970s. The larger of the volumes has an A-frame roof with glass walls beneath. Inside is an elementary space with a range cooker, dining table, and upholstered window seat with views over the valley below. Above are two narrow loft spaces accessed via separate ladders, which provide space for three to sleep.

At the opposite end of the deck, another structure with a steep pent roof contains a spacious bedroom with a floor-to-ceiling window that overlooks the surrounding countryside. The bed is positioned right up against the glass in this Zen-like space, bringing inhabitants as close to the trees as possible, while furniture is kept to a minimum so that the focus is placed on the wildness of the sprawling volcanic landscape.

Page numbers in **bold** refer to
  illustrations.

[1]   BUILT TO FRAME THE FOREST
    © Peter Aaron/OTTO: 52–53; Sean Airhart/Heliotrope Architects: 82–85; Cesar Beja/CO-LAB DESIGN OFFICE: 42–47; Jinnawat Borihankijanan/Napon Jaturapuchapornpong/Prapan Napawongdee/Shma Company Limited: 76–81; Cristobal/Estudio Palma: 72–75; © Joe Fletcher/Faulkner Architects: 20–23; Courtesy of Benjamin G. Saxe and Studio Saxe: 24–29; Andres Garcia/Studio Saxe: 56–61; René Pérez Gómez/Pérez Gómez Arquitectura: 14–19; © Hufton+Crow: 48–51; ©Keith Isaacs: 86–89; Jag Studio: 62–65; Jan Henrik Jansen Arkitekter with Marshall Blecher. with assistance from Einrum Arkitekter: 34–37; © Nic Lehoux: 10–13; Onnis Luque/Productora: 66–71; Raphael Thibodeau/Natalie Dionne: 30–33; Marino Thorlacius/KRADS: 38–41.

[2]   BUILT IN HARMONY WITH THE FOREST
    A-01/Fernando Alda: 156–159; Atelier Marko Brajovic: 142–145; Cesar Bejar/Zeller & Moye: 128–131; Henny van Belkom/Woonpioniers: 122–127; Cristobal/Estudio Palma: 132–135; Roberto Dambrosio/Vida Design: 146–149; DOOK Photos/Nicholas Plewman Architects + Associates, Michaelis Boyd Associates: 160–165; Jan Henrik Jansen Arkitekter with Marshall Blecher; © Daniel Koh: 137, 138–140, 141b; © 2017 Photographix | Sebastian + Ira: 150–153; Miro Pochyba/Y100 ateliér: 100, 102–103; Priidu Saart/B210: 106–107; Sindre Ellingsen/Helen & Hard: 108–113; Pavol Štofan/Y100 ateliér: 101; © takeshi noguchi: 118–121; Fangfang Tiang/ZJJZ: 114–117; Tõnu Tunnel/B210: 104–105; Word of Mouth: 136, 141t.

[3]   BUILT TO BECOME THE FOREST
    Dane Alonso: 234–237; Cesar Bejar: 238–239; Tamás Bujnovszky/Béres Architects: 216–219; Cristobal/Estudio Palma: 248–251; © Dook+ © Visi: 230, 232t; © Bruce Duffy: 198–199, 201; David Dworkind: 184–187; © Florian Busch Architects: 178–183; © Frankie Pappas: 231, 232b, 232; fernando guerra/studio mk27: 94–99, 192–197; instagram @buro511: 212–215; Marc Goodwin, Archmospheres/Studio Puisto Architects: 202–205; © NUDO: 174–179; Primeiro Plano Audiovisual/João Marques Franco: 226–229; © Lara Swimmer Photography: 206–211; Tamarack imagery: 200; Dmitrii Tsyrenshchikov/Horomystudio: 244–247; Paweł Ulatowski/Przemek Olczyk: 188–191; Clinton Weaver/Welsh + Major: 220–225; Marcos Zegers/Iragüen Viñuela Arquitectos: 240–243.

Cover photo: Sindre Ellingsen/Helen & Hard

Phaidon Press Limited
2 Cooperage Yard
London E15 2QR

Phaidon Press Inc.
65 Bleecker Street
New York, NY 10012

phaidon.com

First published 2022
© 2022 Phaidon Press Limited

ISBN 978 1 83866 559 3

A CIP catalogue record for this book is available from the
British Library and the Library of Congress.

Commissioning Editor: Emilia Terragni
Project Editor: Holly Pollard
Production Controller: Gif Jittiwutikarn
Design: SJG/Joost Grootens, Dimitri Jeannottat,
    Julie da Silva
Text: Tessa Pearson

Printed in China

The publisher would like to thank Sarah Bell, Clare Churly,
Lisa Delgado, and Robyn Taylor for their contributions to
the book.